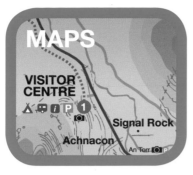

useful maps of Glencoe

the top ten things to see and do in the Glen

a special place

a naturalist's paradise

a geological wonder

the peak of the mountains

KT-162-432

witness to dramatic history

the great outdoors

while you are in the area ...

The top ten things to see and do in the Glen

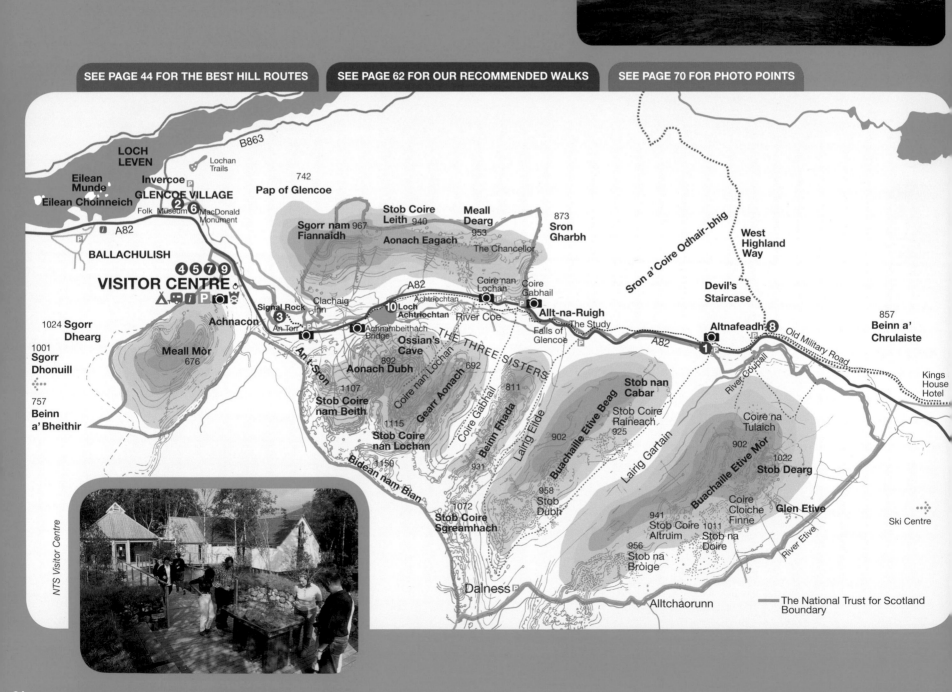

SEE PAGE 44 FOR THE BEST HILL ROUTES

SEE PAGE 62 FOR OUR RECOMMENDED WALKS

SEE PAGE 70 FOR PHOTO POINTS

B863

LOCH LEVEN

Lochan Trails

Eilean Munde

Invercoe

Eilean Choinneich

GLENCOE VILLAGE

Folk Museum

MacDonald Monument

A82

BALLACHULISH

742 **Pap of Glencoe**

Sgorr nam Fiannaidh 967

Stob Coire Leith 940

Meall Dearg 953

Aonach Eagach

The Chancellor

873 **Sron Gharbh**

Sron a' Coire Odhair-bhig

West Highland Way

VISITOR CENTRE

1024 **Sgorr Dhearg**

1001 **Sgorr Dhonuill**

757 **Beinn a' Bheithir**

Meall Mòr 676

Achnacon

Signal Rock

Clachaig Inn

An Torr

A82

Achtriochtan

Achnambeithach Bridge

Loch Achtriochtan

Coire nan Lochan

Coire Gabhail

Allt-na-Ruigh

River Coe

The Study

Falls of Glencoe

Devil's Staircase

Altnafeadh

Old Military Road

857 **Beinn a' Chrulaiste**

An t-Sron

Ossian's Cave

Aonach Dubh 892

THE THREE SISTERS

1107 **Stob Coire nam Beith**

Coire nan Lochan

Gearr Aonach 692

811

1115

Stob Coire nan Lochan

Beinn Fhada

Coire Gabhail

Lairig Eilde

902

Stob nan Cabar

Stob Coire Raineach 925

Buachaille Etive Beag

Coire na Tulaich

902 **Buachaille Etive Mòr**

1022 **Stob Dearg**

1150

Bidean nam Bian

931

958 **Stob Dubh**

Lairig Gartain

River Coupail

Glen Etive

Coire Cloiche Finne

1072 **Stob Coire Sgreamhach**

941 **Stob Coire Altruim**

1011 **Stob na Doire**

956 **Stob na Bròige**

Dalness

Alltchaorunn

River Etive

Ski Centre

Kings House Hotel

— The National Trust for Scotland Boundary

NTS Visitor Centre

While you are in Glencoe, why don't you ...

1 Take a photo from the car park at Lairig Gartain at the east end of the Glen.

2 Visit the Folk Museum in Glencoe village and find out about the area's past.

3 Walk to Signal Rock, the site where a fire would be lit to warn of danger.

4 Explore the Visitor Centre, meet a Ranger and find out everything you need to know about the area.

5 Discover your inner child and solve the children's challenge at the Visitor Centre exhibition.

6 See the monument in Glencoe village to the MacDonalds of Glencoe killed in the Massacre.

7 Stand on the viewing platform at the Visitor Centre and look at an ancient volcano.

8 Take a walk along the West Highland Way to the 'Devil's Staircase' for a fantastic view of Buachaille Etive Mòr.

9 Go on a Land Rover Wildlife Safari with one of the National Trust for Scotland Rangers.

10 Stand in the Glen near to Loch Achtriochtan and look up at Ossian's Cave.

Find out more at www.glencoe-nts.org.uk

'I cannot attempt to describe the mountains. I can only say that [they]…were the grandest I had ever seen. It seldom happens that mountains in a very clear air look exceedingly high, but these, though we could see the whole of them to their very summits, appeared to me more majestic in their own nakedness than our imaginations could have conceived them to be, had they been half hidden by clouds, yet showing some of their highest pinnacles.'

Dorothy Wordsworth, *Journal*, 1803

Glencoe: a special place

Glencoe is internationally famous for its dramatic and extraordinary landscape, for its no less dramatic history, and for its important wildlife. This very special place is in the care of The National Trust for Scotland, which first acquired land here in 1935, and now owns some 5,680 hectares (14,000 acres). It's difficult to sum up this powerful, inspiring, brooding, threatening, fantastic Glen. Throughout this guidebook you will find quotations – often from famous people – demonstrating just some of the passion that Glencoe has aroused over the centuries.

Buzzard (Buteo buteo)

'Emerging from the village we entered the Pass of Glencoe, which at the opening is beautifully green, with trees and cottages dotted about along the verdant valley ... A sharp turn in the rough, very winding, and in some parts precipitous road, brings you to the finest, wildest, and grandest part of the pass. Stern, rugged, precipitous mountains with beautiful peaks and rocks piled high one above the other, two and three thousand feet high, tower and rise up to the heavens on either side, without any signs of habitation ...'

Queen Victoria, *More leaves from the journal of a life in the Highlands*, 1883

Yellow mountain saxifrage
(Saxifraga aizoides)

Travelling by carriage in Glencoe,
c1900

Horatio McCulloch (1805–67): Glencoe

Glencoe:
a naturalist's paradise

'*What better than a Wilderness, to liberate the mind.*'

Stewart Conn, 1995

Glencoe is significant not only for its landscape but for its wildlife, with over fifty rare and special species of flora and fauna. In recognition of this, part of the Glen has been given extra protection as a Special Area of Conservation. It is one of The National Trust for Scotland's most ecologically important outdoor properties and our aim has always been to balance the needs of visitors with the protection of habitats and the variety of plants and animals they support. Since 1935 we have witnessed enormous changes in visitor numbers: today, easier transport, greater leisure time and an increased interest in walking and climbing bring over 2.5 million people to the Glen each year. But this brings added pressure: with one million cars travelling through the Glen annually, lay-bys can quickly become overcrowded. Parking, litter, wild camping and erosion are just some of the issues which the Trust must manage to protect the landscape and habitats of this 'wild land'.

Our approach is underpinned by the Unna Principles, a list of conditions drawn up by mountaineer Percy Unna, the benefactor who helped the Trust to purchase a significant part of Glencoe in the mid-1930s. Scotland in Unna's time was very different from the present day: in the 1930s only the most determined traveller would face a hard day's journey to reach this remote Glen. But Unna had witnessed the urbanising effects of tourist developments in the Alps in the 1930s, and he was concerned that Scotland's mountains should retain their 'primitive' qualities. Unna's recommendations on development still guide the Trust's work in Glencoe today and lie at the heart of the Trust's Wild Land Policy. As part of managing Glencoe to protect its wilderness, no new paths have been created and no signs or waymarkers have been erected on the hills.

The amazing sequence of geological events that created Glencoe left a legacy in the underlying rocks which today provide soil for some of the rarest plants in Britain. From the highest mountain peak, where tiny alpine plants cling to acid soils, to the lime-rich Dalradian rocks that support an abundance of plantlife, Glencoe has a diversity of habitats seen in few other places. The woods that cling to the cliffs are amongst the richest in Britain for mosses and liverworts, and the high mountaintops have a rich arctic-alpine flora. The climate too, with its often wet and windy weather, plays an important part in sustaining habitats from ancient woodland, mountain heath and cliff to peat bog, grassland and loch.

Above, from top: rowan (Sorbus aucuparia)*; red deer* (Cervus elaphus)*; Percy Unna; starry saxifrage* (Saxifraga stellaris)

A question of conservation

The decisions that we make now influence the future of Glencoe. But not all of the choices are straightforward. Nature conservation is a complicated business: by taking action to benefit one species, another may be adversely affected. The Trust's overall aim in managing the natural heritage of Glencoe is to conserve the important habitats and species that are found here, balancing the needs of one group against those of another. Some of the most pressing conservation issues at Glencoe focus on managing grazing, encouraging woodland to regenerate and maintaining access to the mountains for all.

To graze or not to graze?

The way the landscape of Glencoe looks today is a result of a combination of many factors, both human and environmental. But perhaps the biggest single impact on the appearance of Glencoe's landscape is caused by grazing deer and sheep.

Red deer (*Cervus elaphus*) are by choice woodland animals, but over the millennia, as the forests disappeared, they have adapted to life on the open moor. Extremely prolific creatures, the deer population can increase at a rate of thirty per cent each year if left unchecked, and annual culls are carried out to keep their numbers under control. Boundaries mean little to deer, which can roam long distances, jumping cattle fences with ease and grazing freely as they go. A major concern at Glencoe is the serious damage they inflict on trees and shrubs, often preventing the growth of young plants.

Traditionally the other grazing animals in Glencoe were cattle and sheep. For about a thousand years cattle were the dominant domestic stock grazing the area. During the summer months, villagers would move with their cattle to the 'shielings' at Kingshouse and on Meall Mòr to enjoy the lush grazing further up the Glen. Today there are only about twenty cattle and 500 sheep in the Glen.

Grazing animals, like deer and sheep, determine which plants grow partly by their preference for certain species and partly by the plants' response to being grazed. Add to that the seasonal element that the effect of grazing on plants varies at different times of the year – when a plant is actively growing, flowering or setting seed, it may be more easily damaged than at other times – and it becomes clear that conservation management involves constant monitoring, evaluation and adjustment.

Grazing is an important part of our upland ecology and influences the type of plants that can grow. Some habitats, like the flower-rich grasslands which thrive on the lime-rich soil of Meall Mòr, require grazing for their conservation, while others, such as the extensive areas of mountain fern on the hill slopes, do not. In areas where we want to encourage heather or young trees and shrubs to grow, we are reducing the amount of grazing by red deer and sheep. And in certain areas, for instance where we are trying to regenerate the mountain willows, there is no grazing at all. A combination of minimal fencing to protect pockets of habitat from grazing, shepherding of sheep and maintaining sustainable numbers of deer helps us to achieve this important balance.

A study of the Scots pine at Glen Etive found that the heavy grazing of deer was repressing the growth of around eighty trees, many of them seedlings. The construction of an enclosure around the remaining trees is helping them to naturally regenerate.

A wooded glen?

At the end of the last Ice Age, about 11,000 years ago, woodland cover increased in upland Scotland. But in the millennia that followed, through natural and man-induced causes, the amount of woodland declined.

One of the conservation questions facing the Trust today is how much native woodland is appropriate for Glencoe. This question is further complicated by our limited knowledge of just how wooded the Glen was in the past and the modern acceptance of Glencoe as an area characterised by open vistas across treeless moorland. To help manage this major conservation concern we have zoned the property, identifying areas where the landscape should remain open together with areas of existing woodland which we would like to regenerate. Taking place over many decades, regeneration of native woodland is a very gradual process. The trees are not planted, but rather are allowed to seed themselves. This maintains the wild and natural qualities which are so important at Glencoe.

Areas of native woodland still exist in Glencoe: native birch trees grow on the mountain crags, on Meall Mòr mountain willows thrive, at Achnacon there is a native alder wood and to the east of Glencoe, at Glen Etive, an important remnant of Scots pine survives. To encourage these species to regenerate we are restricting grazing by creating exclosures to keep deer and sheep out, while allowing access for walkers via stiles.

Glencoe tree & shrub list
(based on property as a whole; may be locally common)

Trees

Acer pseudoplatanus	Sycamore	Rare *Not native*
Alnus glutinosa	Alder	Common on riversides
Betula pubescens	Downy birch	Common
Fraxinus excelsior	Ash	Uncommon
Picea sitchensis	Sitka spruce	An Torr plantation *Not native*
Pinus sylvestris	Scots pine	Rare
Populus tremula	Aspen	Rare
Prunus avium	Gean	Very rare
Prunus padus	Bird cherry	Very rare (gorges)
Quercus petraea	Sessile oak	Rare
Ulmus glabra	Wych elm	Very rare (gorges)

Shrubs

Corylus avellana	Hazel	Rare
Crataegus monogyna	Hawthorn	Rare
Ilex aquifolium	Holly	Rare
Salix aurita	Eared willow	Uncommon
Salix caprea	Goat willow	Rare
Salix cinerea	Grey willow	Uncommon
Salix phylicifolia	Tea-leaved willow	Rare
Sorbus aucuparia	Rowan	Uncommon

Dwarf shrubs

Calluna vulgaris	Heather	Abundant
Erica cinerea	Bell heather	Abundant
Erica tetralix	Cross-leaved heath	Common
Myrica gale	Bog myrtle	Common
Salix herbacea	Dwarf willow	Uncommon (summits)
Salix myrsinites	Whortle-leaved willow	Rare
Salix repens	Creeping willow	Uncommon

Access for all

Ever since The National Trust for Scotland acquired Glencoe in the 1930s, we have maintained a policy of open access to the mountains at all times. Our role in conserving the environment has never been more vital, as increasing numbers of walkers and climbers together with the steep terrain and wet weather combine to cause serious erosion on the mountains.

With at least 150,000 walkers and climbers each year on the mountains of Glencoe, human traffic inevitably takes its toll. One consequence is that over the years the pounding of many pairs of boots has created a network of footpaths. This continual footfall wears through the thin vegetation, exposing soils and sub-soils to the erosive powers of rain. Many walkers then take to the path edges where it is more comfortable to walk. In doing so they set in motion further erosion as the path edges wear down, producing an ever-expanding and intrusive scar on the landscape.

With 65 km (40 miles) of footpaths in the Glencoe mountains, footpath maintenance is a key area of conservation work for the Trust. Our main work aims to counter erosion by stabilising slopes, shedding water from paths and encouraging walkers to stay on the renewed path surface to allow the bare, eroded ground to regenerate. At a cost of between £30 and £100 to repair a one-metre stretch of footpath in the Glen and £250 to construct a cross drain, the process of footpath maintenance is expensive and labour-intensive. In the last fifteen years we have spent in the region of £2 million on footpath repairs throughout our properties. The Trust is always grateful for donations to this work through its Sole Trading Appeal.

One of the intractable yet fascinating aspects of countryside management is deciding the best way to care for a particular place. For many years, the Trust has repaired the major landscape scars caused by path erosion within the Glen. With the development of new low-impact path management techniques, such repairs are hardly noticeable to the average walker. The improved surfaces keep walkers on the path-line and prevent the spread of erosion – but they can also make it easier for mountaineers to access more remote ground. It can be argued that, to a degree, this compromises the special wild qualities of Glencoe.

W 208 532

'The Glen means so much to me. I, for one, respect and value the great glen of Glencoe. Imagine being at the top of a mountain on a bright and breezy day, the birds chirping, the sheep grazing, the cries of children playing and the joy of being free – what a wonderful feeling of freedom. I can experience this any day living in the Glen. I hope you will learn to value the Glen as much as I.'

Iain R Brown, age 11, Glencoe Primary School

Wonderful wildlife

The many different types of habitat in Glencoe, from wetland and woodland to moorland and mountain, support a great variety of wildlife. Moorland and mountain slopes are home to our largest native land mammal, **red deer**, which were originally forest-dwelling animals, but adapted, as the wooded areas declined, to roaming the moors of Glencoe. Romanticised as the 'monarch of the glen', deer are magnificent animals, but when their numbers get too high they can damage woodland and destroy young trees. With no natural predator to keep their population in check, management of red deer is an important issue at Glencoe.

Another, more elusive, creature, the **pine marten**, has also adapted to live on the cliffs and scree slopes of the Glen. They almost disappeared from Glencoe a hundred years ago because much of their woodland habitat was cleared for grazing. A further threat came from hunters who trapped the animals for their valuable fur. Fully protected by law since 1988, their numbers are now beginning to stabilise.

The work that The National Trust for Scotland is carrying out in Glencoe to regenerate native woodland is good news for one of our tiniest mammals. Measuring only four centimetres long and weighing less than a two pence coin, the **pipistrelle bat** feeds in wooded areas of the Glen, eating up to an astonishing 3,000 insects in a night. Many other animals make their home here too, from otters, foxes, moles and badgers to roe deer, voles and weasels.

Pine marten (Martes martes)

Northern water vole (Arvicola terrestris)

Red deer (Cervus elaphus)

016

Wildcat
Felis sylvestris grampia
A nocturnal animal that is now rarely seen in Glencoe. Its numbers declined dramatically in previous centuries and today it is a protected species. In the UK it is found only in Scotland. The main threats to its survival come from interbreeding with domestic cats and persecution by humans.

Mountain hare
Lepus timidus
This species arrived in Scotland about 11,000 years ago at the end of the Ice Age. It lives on the high moors in Glencoe, where it feeds on heather. In winter the hare's coat turns from grey-brown to white, camouflaging it against the snow. Numbers are declining in the Glen, which may be related to the wet climate.

Atlantic salmon
Salmo salar
The numbers of Atlantic salmon that spawn in Glencoe's freshwater rivers are greatly in decline, possibly due to pollution and maladies owing to infestations of sea-lice. We are helping to restore the salmon's natural habitat by trying to keep rivers free from pollutants caused by industry and agriculture and from other man-made obstructions that can impede the salmon's migration.

Marsh fritillary butterfly
Eurodryas aurinia
This rare butterfly lives in the marshy grasslands of Glencoe. Its caterpillars feed on a plant called devil's-bit scabious. To help protect this butterfly we are allowing the grassland areas to thrive and are lowering grazing pressure from deer and sheep.

Roe deer (Capreolus capreolus)

Otter (Lutra lutra)

Fantastic flora

The rocky outcrops of lime-rich calcareous rocks on the mountain tops, cliffs and ledges of Glencoe support a number of very important arctic-alpine plants, including nationally scarce species, like **Highland saxifrage** and **Alpine saxifrage**. Most of the hillsides are underlain by hard, acidic rocks which give rise to the sweeping moorland so often associated with the Highlands. Plants like **bell heather**, **tormentil** and **bracken** flourish in the drier areas, while **cross-leaved heath**, **sundews** and **bog asphodel** grow in the wet heathland, bog and marsh. Lower down the Glen in the area below The Three Sisters, an internationally important group of **mosses** and **liverworts** thrive. Known as **oceanic bryophytes**, these plants are found only in cool, humid and unpolluted areas, making the west of Scotland one of the most important places in the world for them.

Harebell or Scottish bluebell (Campanula rotundifolia)

Dog violet (Viola riviniana)

Bog moss (Sphagnum capillifolium)

Main image: Bog asphodel (Narthecium ossifragum)

Roseroot (Sedum rosea)

Butterwort (Pinguicula vulgaris) *with insects caught on its sticky leaves*

Heath spotted orchid
(Dactylorhiza maculata)

Purple saxifrage (Saxifraga oppositifolia)

Round-leaved sundew (Drosera rotundifolia)

Ling or common heather
(Calluna vulgaris)

Yellow mountain saxifrage
(Saxifraga aizoides)

Whortle-leaved willow
Salix myrsinites
This sub-arctic plant is a rare species that grows on ungrazed ledges high up on the Glencoe mountains. To protect it from being eaten and destroyed by sheep we have fenced around the main areas where it grows.

Liverwort
Herbertus aduncus
This liverwort grows in birch woods below The Three Sisters and is one of the commonest of the oceanic bryophyte flora found only in western Britain. Environmentally, it is an indicator of habitat condition, as any change in water, soil or air quality has an impact on its growth.

Tormentil (Potentilla erecta)

Mountain avens
Dryas octopetala
This grows in only one area in Glencoe, on the lime-rich soil of Meall Mòr. One of the first 'pioneer' plants to take root soon after the end of the Ice Age, this beautiful plant needs balanced grazing – enough to keep down the tall grasses that would otherwise choke it, but not so much that it is eaten away. We are carefully managing sheep grazing on Meall Mòr, to ensure that the mountain avens can flourish.

Beautiful birds

Perhaps some of the most visible forms of wildlife in Glencoe are the birds, which, with their grace, freedom and mobility, make fascinating watching. In the remoter parts of the Glen, powerful **peregrine falcons**, soaring **buzzards**, hovering **kestrels** and slender **merlins** are all regularly seen flying above the mountains. The **golden eagle**, one of the largest and most spectacular birds of prey, regularly hunts in Glencoe. On the very highest mountaintops **ptarmigan** and **snow buntings** seem to thrive against all odds in the arctic-like climate.

On the moorlands **red grouse** roam, and **ring ouzels** and **golden plover** visit to breed during the summer months. The woodlands of Glencoe are particularly valuable habitats, providing food and shelter for **owls**, **sparrowhawks**, **coal tits**, **warblers**, **woodpeckers**, **goldcrests** and **chaffinches**. Lower down in the marshes and around Loch Achtriochtan, wetland birds like **mallard** and **goldeneye ducks**, **grey herons**, **whooper swans**, **redshanks**, **dippers** and **wigeons** can be seen.

Much of our conservation work centres on maintaining suitable habitat and breeding conditions for birds, particularly those of high national conservation concern because of their declining populations. For the ring ouzel we are working to ensure that there is no further loss of its habitat; for the **skylark** we are retaining areas of long grassland to provide suitable nesting cover; and for the **song thrush** we are promoting farming and woodland practices which are sensitive to the birds' needs, including avoiding the use of pesticides.

(1) *Mallard* (Anas platyrhynchos)
(2) *Whooper swans* (Cygnus cygnus)
(3) *Red grouse* (Lagopus lagopus scoticus)
(4) *Greater-spotted woodpecker* (Dendrocopos major)
(5) *Goldeneye* (Bucephala clangula)

Main image: Golden eagle (Aquila chrysaetos)

How you can help to secure the future of Glencoe

- follow the Scottish Outdoor Access Code (www.outdooraccess-scotland.com)
- keep to footpaths
- leave rocks and stones untouched
- leave plants and flowers growing for all to enjoy
- keep rivers and lochs free from pollution
- avoid lighting fires or dropping matches
- become a member of The National Trust for Scotland

'I have been living in Scotland for just over three years. When I first came into Glencoe village all I saw was a huge, wide area of space bordered with mountains and wildlife. I then travelled into the heart of the village where there were lots of small cosy houses, with groups of children laughing and playing. I heard birds chirping and a small, cool, refreshing breeze on my face. After that gust of wind I knew this place was the most lively, fun-filled place I had been in, for my entire life. I personally love the Glen. I enjoy the fresh air and all the wildlife spaced around. Fun-filled natural wonders is what the Glen means to me. What does it mean to you?'

Rhea Wood, age 11, Glencoe Primary School

Peregrine falcon
Falco peregrinus
Nests on the remote rocky crags of Glencoe, and feeds on other birds including crows, grouse and pigeons. You can sometimes see it making almost vertical dives as it swoops on its prey. In recent years the main threats to the falcon have come from toxic chemicals like DDT, which wreak havoc with their ability to breed, and from wildlife crime including illegal egg collecting.

Ring ouzel
Turdus torquatus
Similar to blackbirds, ring ouzels tend to be shy birds which visit Glencoe to breed during the spring and summer months. They are found on the open moorland and amongst the crags, gullies and boulders of the mountains. The rapid decline in the UK breeding population over the last twenty-five years has placed them on the Red List of birds of high conservation concern. We are working to ensure that their habitat is protected.

Ptarmigan
Lagopus mutus
A member of the grouse family, the ptarmigan lives on the very highest mountain peaks of Glencoe. In winter its feathers provide camouflage by turning snow-white, helping to protect it from predators. As ptarmigan can survive only in very cold conditions, global warming is one of the main threats to the species.

Glencoe: a geological wonder

Looking down Coire Gabhail

'What happens to us
Is irrelevant to the world's geology
But what happens to the world's geology
Is not irrelevant to us.
We must reconcile ourselves to the stones,
Not the stones to us.'

Hugh MacDiarmid, 1934

In the beginning ...

The grandeur of Glencoe, with its towering mountains and ice-gouged glen, rarely fails to arouse our emotions. Perhaps this is because it gives us a sense of connecting with a primeval past, for its rocks tell a story that reaches back more than 500 million years, long before dinosaurs roamed the Earth, when shallow seas gave way to tall mountains, when huge volcanoes dominated the landscape and when only primitive plants and algae populated mainly barren slopes and ephemeral pools.

Glencoe's secret history

- 500 million years ago, Scotland lay on a separate continent from England.

- Fossil spores found in rocks at Glencoe indicate that primitive plants clung precariously to the barren wasteland here 420 million years ago.

- Over a period of five million years, violent volcanoes tore through and buried the land around Glencoe. The volcanic rocks of Glencoe show evidence of at least eight massive eruptions.

- The rocks at Glencoe, including the volcanic rocks, bear witness to many different environments: some were formed on the floor of a shallow sea, and others in sub-tropical deserts. All were ground down under the base of a vast ice sheet.

- Today Glencoe bears open wounds where recent huge rockfalls and exceptionally active screes combine to make this one of the most dynamically changing landscapes in Britain.

Top right: a Ranger points towards Aonach Eagach

Above: local geologist Jim Blair takes a group through the Glen, explaining how it was formed

Right: one of the many huge boulders still standing precariously where melting glaciers dumped them at the end of the Ice Age

Stob Dubh from Stob Coire Raineach

Mighty mountains emerge

About 500 million years ago Scotland lay next to Newfoundland and Greenland on the ancient continent of Laurentia. England was part of the small continent of Avalonia, and the two continents were separated by the Iapetus Ocean, wider than the present-day Atlantic. Then, as now, the giant plates that form the Earth's crust were in constant motion. Over a period of 70 million years, these great continental plates, powered by slow-flowing currents deep within the hot rock of the Earth's mantle, drifted together, narrowing the ocean that lay between.

Around 470 million years ago, a period of extraordinary upheaval and violent movement changed the face of the Earth and initiated the mountain building that we recognise in the geology of today's landscape. This was the time of Caledonian mountain building, when dynamic forces consumed the ocean and lifted the rocks of the continents thousands of metres above sea level to form the mighty Caledonian Mountains. These mountains, which stretch from the Appalachians of eastern North America to northern Scandinavia, may have towered some four times higher than the mountains of Glencoe today.

By 430 million years ago, as fish, the first back-boned animals, were evolving, the huge geological plates carrying the ancient continents of Laurentia, Baltica and Avalonia had collided.

This new continent formed by the welding of Laurentia and Avalonia lay in the southern hemisphere, with Glencoe positioned about 20° south of the equator; the climate was semi-arid with heavy seasonal rainfall, similar to that of present-day western Africa. The newly formed mountains of Glencoe comprised bare rocks, uplifted from where they had been laid down on the coastal plains and seabed surrounding Laurentia, and folded and metamorphosed in the process. These rocks are termed the Dalradian. With little soil or plant cover, they eroded rapidly in flash floods, depositing huge quantities of sediment in the valleys and flood plains within the emerging mountain chain.

Rannoch Moor

Buachaille Etive Beag

500 million years ago

Scotland was part of the ancient continent of Laurentia, which also included North America, Greenland and the north of Ireland.

England, Wales and the south of Ireland were part of a different continent called Avalonia. The huge Iapetus Ocean separated the two continents.

A third continent, Baltica, included present-day Scandinavia and Russia.

440 - 420 million years ago

Over millions of years the Iapetus Ocean narrowed and the continents eventually collided. Where the ocean had once been, the massive Caledonian Mountains formed, the ancient heart of present-day Glencoe.

○ position of Scotland

| 500 million years ago CAMBRIAN | 430 million years ago SILURIAN | 400 million years ago DEVONIAN | 300 million years ago CARBONIFEROUS |

LAURENTIA BALTICA IAPETUS OCEAN AVALONIA GONDWANA

| 260 million years ago PERMIAN | 200 million years ago JURASSIC | 65 million years ago CRETACEOUS | present day |

Violent volcanoes erupt

' ... it is, like all the wild mountains of Scotland, a lesson in humility. Man has never existed for it; it is, at least in sunlight, not unfriendly so much as utterly oblivious of humanity ... Here is a landscape without mercy. So far as Glencoe is concerned the first germ of life has never struggled from the warm slime. It is still dreaming of geological convulsions.'

H V Morton, *In Search of Scotland*, 1929

As the internal engine of the Earth continued to churn, movements in the Earth's crust caused deep faults to appear. We know from sedimentary rocks within the volcanic pile that an ancient river flowed north-westwards through the Glencoe area, following the line of weakness along a major fault. Other faults cut across this valley, reaching down to chambers of molten magma beneath the Earth's surface. Along the faults, blocks of the Earth's crust subsided. Hugely explosive eruptions blasted the very innards of the Earth sky-high in massive columns of ash, pumice and crystals. As this incandescent mixture, which reached temperatures of 800-1000°C, collapsed back down to Earth, it surged across the landscape in red-hot flows, which cooled quickly to form rock known as ignimbrite. Many of the mountains of Glencoe, like Buachaille Etive Mòr and Buachaille Etive Beag, are formed in part from these rocks which, together with the distinctively fractured rhyolite and andesite, provide some of the best climbing crags in the area.

The cataclysmic volcanic activity that occurred at Glencoe 420 million years ago probably lasted for a period of about five million years. During this time at least eight major volcanic eruptions occurred, each of which displaced tens to hundreds of cubic kilometres of magma from inside the Glencoe volcano. During each eruption, which may have lasted only days or even hours, the unsupported roof of the magma chamber sagged and collapsed piecemeal along the major fault lines, forming a 'caldera', a huge basin-like hole at the surface, eventually extending to some 14 kilometres across. Later in the history of Glencoe, after much of the volcanic activity had ceased, magma flowed into the fault lines and also between the volcanic rocks, where it solidified to form the so-called ring intrusions that now surround the volcanic rocks, and the large granite mass (pluton) within.

Today, our understanding of the processes of caldera collapse has advanced from the simplistic yet influential models of volcano development that were first developed a hundred years ago in Glencoe, but the ancient volcano still has secrets to reveal to painstaking geological study and help us to understand the formation of these huge volcanic depressions. Over the millions of years since the caldera-volcano formed, hundreds of metres of volcanic rocks have been removed by ice, wind and rain; what we see today is a superb record of ancient volcanic eruptions fortuitously preserved by caldera collapse.

A member of the NTS Young Naturalists' Club interacts with a model of a volcanic eruption that occurred at Glencoe some 420 million years ago

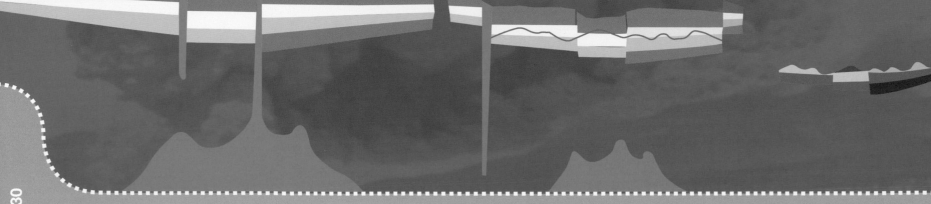

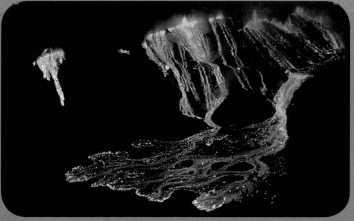

Each of the cataclysmic explosive eruptions at Glencoe was of a scale not witnessed in modern times; they were accompanied by tremendous earthquakes and must have affected the ancient climate. The photograph above shows a small-scale modern counterpart of what happened at Glencoe. A huge umbrella-cloud of ash darkens the sky while incandescent hot flows of ash, pumice and crystals tear across the landscape at speeds up to 120 miles per hour (55 metres per second). No life survives in the path of these deadly pyroclastic flows

The photograph on the left shows lava at temperatures over 1000ºC cascading from a fissure-vent into a lava-lake beneath. The mighty buttresses of Bidean nam Bian and Stob Coire nan Lochan are made of andesite that was also erupted along fissures and originally formed a lava-lake inside Glencoe caldera. Unique in the world, the ancient lava-lake at Glencoe was hundreds of metres deep and the 'fire fountains' that fed it would have been immense. Few climbers suspect that the sheer columns of rock they scale on these lofty peaks were formed by the cooling of a huge lake of lava

Inexorable ice erodes

Whilst we may marvel that the mountains of Glencoe stand testament to the volcanoes that exploded here 420 million years ago, in reality this active volcanic landscape bore very little resemblance to the glen we now know. The peaks and valleys of Glencoe owe far more to the glaciers and ice sheets that sculpted them over the last two million years. In the millions of years that followed the period of volcanic activity at Glencoe, the land that became Scotland gradually drifted northward through desert and sub-tropical climates until, at the start of the Ice Age two and a half million years ago, it lay close to its present position, 56° north of the equator.

Looking up the River Coe from An Torr, near Signal Rock: Aonach Eagach is on the left, Aonach Dubh on the right

Coire Gabhail, looking (left) towards and (above) away from Bidean nam Bian: gravel is trapped here by huge rocks that have blocked the valley entrance for thousands of years

As the Ice Age tightened its arctic grip over Scotland, a succession of glaciations gouged and scoured through the Glen, shaping the spectacular mountains of Glencoe over a period of two million years. In the last major glaciation, 29,000 to 14,700 years ago, ice blanketed most of Britain. In Glencoe the ice formed a massive sheet some 1,000 metres thick, from which only the tops of the highest mountains protruded. This colossal ice sheet eventually melted as the climate became wet and mild, similar to our climate today. But ice returned to Glencoe again. About 12,500 years ago glaciers flowed out from an ice cap that had accumulated at the site that is now the wilderness of Rannoch Moor, to the east of Glencoe. From here a glacier flowed down the Glen to the sea at Loch Linnhe, filling it to a height of 650 metres. The erosive power of the ice, far greater than any river, gouged out rock from the valley walls and sculpted the deep U-shape that characterises the Glen today.

As the climate finally warmed 11,500 years ago, the ice cap shrank and the glaciers retreated, leaving huge rocks and piles of gravel behind them. As the glaciers disappeared, massive buttresses, loosened by ice high up on one of The Three Sisters, collapsed, blocking the entrance to the hanging valley of Coire Gabhail, hiding it from the main glen. Later, this feature became a favourite hiding place of the MacDonalds for stolen cattle. Today the ground within Coire Gabhail is covered with sheets of gravel brought down the mountain slopes by rivers, unable to be carried any further because of the huge rocks blocking the entrance to the valley.

The geology of Glencoe reveals a dramatic history of continents colliding, oceans disappearing, volcanoes erupting and ice eroding, but the area's story does not end there. Glencoe remains one of the most dynamic geological landscapes in Britain. Constant freeze and thaw loosens rocks and sends them hurtling down the mountainsides; scree and rivers etch deep gullies into the softer rocks on the hillsides, taking eroded rocks with them and dumping them at the base of the slopes. Very gradually this mountainous region is being reshaped.

A guide to the rocks

The mountains of Glencoe are formed from six main types of rocks. The oldest rocks, known as Dalradian, started life as seabed sediments some 700 million years ago. When they were crumpled and heated during the Caledonian mountain building, they were metamorphosed to various schists and hard white quartzites. Today, when you look up at the mountains, most of the rocks that you see are ancient volcanic ashes and lavas erupted some 420 million years ago; the metamorphic rocks lie beneath these.

① Dalradian schist — *Shiny grey, banded rock with folded layers*
- **How old?** 700 million years
- **Formed** From sands, silts and limy muds on the edge of the ancient continent of Laurentia. Deformed and altered by huge forces during the Caledonian mountain building.
- **See it** On Meall Mòr, near Loch Achtriochtan and on the hill slopes and coasts around Glencoe and Ballachulish villages.

② Rhyolite — *Pink-coloured rock often with swirling bands, patterns formed by the flow of the magma*
- **How old?** 420 million years
- **Formed** Originally sheets of sticky magma, which erupted from the Glencoe volcanoes in explosive fountains and then flowed out to cover a wide area. An angular jointed rock, particularly suited to climbing.
- **See it** High on The Three Sisters, in Coire Gabhail, from the Study, near the Falls of Glencoe and on Stob Dearg.

③ Andesite — *Grey-purple rock, commonly streaky and with large black or white crystals*
- **How old?** 420 million years
- **Formed** Magma that in places was squeezed up in between wet sands near the Earth's surface, forming layers (sills), and elsewhere flooded into the Glencoe caldera, forming vast, incandescent lava lakes.
- **See it** On the lower slopes of The Three Sisters, especially on the Coire nam Beith path, and forming the summits of Bidean nam Bian and Stob Coire nan Lochan.

④ Granite — *Coarse grained pink and grey rock*
- **How old?** 420 million years
- **Formed** When magma solidified slowly beneath the Earth's surface, forming large crystals.
- **See it** In Glen Etive and in the river near the Clachaig Inn.

⑤ Ignimbrite — *Streaky, banded, grey rock with angular volcanic fragments and with streaks, known as flamme, representing flattened pumice.*
- **How old?** 420 million years
- **Formed** From the deposits left by hot pyroclastic flows during huge caldera-forming eruptions
- **See it** In Coire nam Beitheach, Stob nan Cabar and in the Cam Ghleann.

⑥ Tuff — *Rock made of beds of volcanic ash and rubble*
- **How old?** 420 million years
- **Formed** Thrown out of the Glencoe volcano during powerful explosions; beds record pyroclastic flows and ash fallout from eruption clouds.
- **See it** On the exposed cliffs of Stob Dearg.

A cross-section through the Glen

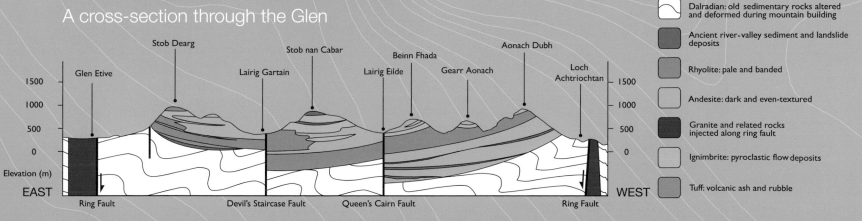

Legend:
- Dalradian: old sedimentary rocks altered and deformed during mountain building
- Ancient river-valley sediment and landslide deposits
- Rhyolite: pale and banded
- Andesite: dark and even-textured
- Granite and related rocks injected along ring fault
- Ignimbrite: pyroclastic flow deposits
- Tuff: volcanic ash and rubble

Glencoe: the peak of the mountains

The dramatic landscape with its vertiginous mountains, radiating ridges and deeply trenched corries has earned Glencoe an international reputation as an outstanding area for rock and ice climbing. With eight Munros (mountains of 3,000 feet/914 metres and over), and ten subsidiary summits over 3,000 feet, the area attracts upwards of 150,000 mountaineers and hill-walkers each year. Over the last century and a half, some of the great names in mountaineering history have pushed the boundaries of their sport ever further on the rocks of Glencoe.

The astronaut Jeffrey Hoffman reflected before the 1985 mission aboard the Space Shuttle Discovery: *'You cannot stay on the summit forever. You have to come down again. So why bother in the first place? Just this: what is above knows what is below, but what is below does not know what is above ... When one can no longer see, one can at least still know.'*

'The silence in recognition of greatness is the silence of people looking at stars or mountains.'
Elspeth Davie, 1995

The Scottish Mountaineering Club meet at Glencoe, Easter 1936. Among the group are Norman Collie (1); Harold Raeburn (2); Hugh Munro (3); and William Naismith (4)

Background: Kings House Hotel and Buachaille Etive Mòr in the 1950s

W H Murray

William Naismith (on right) about 1890

For many, the quest of knowing is the driving force to reach ever greater summits. The formative moment in the career of the legendary mountaineer **W H (William Hutchison) Murray** was overhearing a conversation between two climbers describing an ascent to a narrow rocky ridge when the clouds suddenly cleared to reveal a vista of sea and mountains. For Murray, it was the inspiration he needed to investigate a world of which he knew nothing. For others it is the unadulterated excitement, adrenaline, fear and hope or simply the sheer physical test of strength and endurance.

In 1890 when **Sir Hugh Munro** compiled his list of 'Munros', he could have had little idea of the trend he would launch. The same year the newly formed Scottish Mountaineering Club published the list and Munro-bagging, as we know it today, began. Glencoe in the late nineteenth century was not an easy place to reach: the steam train north terminated at Oban and it was not until 1894 that the railway line to Fort William opened. Motor cars were few and far between and many relied on the horse-drawn Ballachulish and Glencoe stagecoach. But despite the problems of reaching the area, some of the most famous Victorian mountaineers, like **Norman Collie**, **William Wilson Naismith** and **Harold Raeburn**, returned again and again to Glencoe, attempting some of the finest rock and ice climbs to be found in Scotland. Routes such as Crowberry Direct on Buachaille Etive Mòr and Flake Route on Bidean nam Bian went down as classics in mountaineering history and established Glencoe as the spiritual home of Scottish mountaineering.

In the centuries before any mountaineer donned his hobnailed boots, the mountains of Glencoe were the province of the people living in the Glen. It is only in the last 150 years that scaling the peaks has become a leisure activity and, more recently, a sport. The first recorded ascent in Glencoe was in 1868 by **Neil Marquis**, a local shepherd, who made history by climbing Ossian's Ladder to reach the cave on the north face of Aonach Dubh (***please note this climb is dangerous***). The route was not one that was highly rated by later climbers and an article published in 1896 expounded: *'Hands, knees, toes and eyelids had to be awkwardly spread over a mixture of mud and vegetable, which affords a support as treacherous as it is dirty, and which no respectable mountaineer, having regard to his Norfolk, will care to depend on.'*

The Norfolk in question was a warm tweed jacket which, together with baggy knee breeches and a length of hemp rope, was the essential kit of the early rock climber in Glencoe. The rope was often more of a psychological prop than a real aid, being used to tie climbers together rather than anchor them to the rock. It was not until later that rope was threaded into chockstones to help to hold the climber if he lost his footing. Hobnailed boots were the footwear of the day, enabling climbers to grip through mud, moss and lichen in all weathers. On occasion, boots would be removed and the climbers would proceed over very delicate ground in their stockinged feet. Later, hobnailed boots were shod with tricounis, special soft metal nails which could be easily replaced. Some of the early climbs in Glencoe are all the more remarkable given the limited equipment and footwear available in the early 1900s.

Sir Hugh Munro

Harold Raeburn

Abraham's Ledge on Crowberry Ridge, Buachaille Etive Mòr, first ascended by the Abraham brothers in May 1900

Jock Nimlin, a member of the Creagh Dhu Club, on top of Buttress Pinnacle on the Aonach Eagach ridge above Loch Achtriochtan, around 1930

Despite the many obstacles, the early pioneers of the 1900s firmly established Glencoe as one of the premier mountain-climbing areas in Britain. Routes like Crowberry Gully on Buachaille Etive Mòr, climbed by **Harold Raeburn** in 1909, were so far ahead of their time that they went unrepeated for a quarter of a century. But the outbreak of World War I brought mountaineering in the Glen to an abrupt halt. With many climbers killed in active service, it was almost a decade after the war ended before a new generation of mountaineers began to emerge. When mountaineering did begin to take off again in the 1920s it was with a renewed enthusiasm, spurred on by the publication of climbing guidebooks and the formation of groups like the **Junior Mountaineering Club of Scotland** and the **Ptarmigan Club**. Equipment, too, was improving, mainly due to the Everest expeditions of the inter-war years. Lighter, longer and thinner ropes enabled greater runouts to be made and plimsoles, bought from Woolworths, were the new state-of-the-art footwear for harder rock climbs.

The construction of the new Glencoe road in 1931 opened up the area to many more climbers. In its early years, mountaineering had been the preserve of the middle and upper classes, but from the 1930s onwards the class distinctions of the pre-war decades began to erode. One group in particular radically changed the face of Scottish mountaineering at this time. They were the members of the **Creagh Dhu Club**. Formed by workers from Clydebank, the Creagh Dhu found an escape from the hard slog of the shipyards and factories in the mountains of Glencoe, and were pivotal in bringing a new generation of climbers to the Glen with a fresh spirit of competition. **Dennis Gray**, who regularly climbed with the Creagh Dhu, recalled:

'This was a golden era for the Dhus and on my journey with them I grew to appreciate fully the initiative of working-class climbers in escaping from the awful inner-city environment, which appeared then to be a sea of slums and saloon bars, terribly depressing to a newcomer. But there was nothing depressed about my gregarious Glasgow friends, who joked and sang all the way to Arrochar. Every Dhu sported a flat cap, and they looked like the original No Mean City gang.'

Archive photographs of Scottish Mountaineering Club members in action in Glencoe. Anti-clockwise from top right: in 1891; 1894; and on Crowberry Ridge, Buachaille Etive Mòr, in 1927

How Hamish was hooked

It was a chance encounter with a Creagh Dhu climber that launched the career of one of Scotland's best-known mountaineers. As a young man living in Greenock, Hamish MacInnes noticed that his neighbour, Bill Hargreaves, disappeared on his motorbike every weekend. One brief encounter later, MacInnes was perched on the pillion of Hargreaves' bike heading north for his first climbing taste of Glencoe. He was hooked. MacInnes would go on to put up many daring first ascents in Glencoe such as Agag's Groove and Raven's Gully in winter, both on Buachaille Etive Mòr, as well as attempting a daring ascent of Everest in 1953 with fellow Creagh Dhu, John Cunningham. In addition to his legendary resourcefulness as a climber, Hamish MacInnes brought his engineering background to the mountains and was responsible for many technological advances in climbing equipment. As a mountain rescuer, coming across a climbing party who had died on Ben Nevis was a formative moment for MacInnes: '*These climbers had been attempting Zero Gully. The wooden axes were broken when we found the bodies. That made me resolve to get my all-metal axe manufactured.*'
His invention of the first all-metal ice axe and his 'Terrordactyl' ice climbing tool, which he pioneered from his workshop in Glencoe, revolutionised mountain safety on steep ice climbs. Now – equipped with an ice axe in each hand and a pair of front point crampons – climbers could make faster and safer progress on ice and snow. Before long many manufacturers took up MacInnes's original idea and today virtually all ice axes have metal shafts.

Percy Unna (second from right) climbing in Switzerland, July 1925

For many who had taken the freedom of the mountains for granted, the mid-1930s was an unsettling time – Lord Strathcona had put first the Glencoe, then the Dalness Estate up for sale. One man in particular was concerned about the possible fate of the mountains he had grown to love. He was **Percy Unna**, an experienced mountaineer who had climbed both in Scotland and the Alps and was then the President of the Scottish Mountaineering Club. Through his involvement with the Club, Unna met climbers who were supporters of the newly formed National Trust for Scotland, and he in turn became interested in the Trust's work. Determined to prevent possible commercial exploitation, Unna resolved to raise funds to help buy the Glen. Through his work and his own anonymous donations, Unna was instrumental in enabling The National Trust for Scotland to acquire a significant part of Glencoe, safeguarding its outstanding mountain heritage and ensuring access to the mountains for generations of climbers and walkers.

Mountaineering in Glencoe took another leap forward at the end of World War II. **W H Murray's book of 1947**, ***Mountaineering in Scotland***, was hugely influential in popularising the activity and his follow-up guide to Glencoe opened up the area to even more climbers. The Creagh Dhu was still prominent, but a new younger generation was also cutting a dash on the mountainside. In addition to **Hamish MacInnes**, **Jimmy Marshall**, **Dougal Haston**, **Pat Walsh** and **Robin Smith** all made history in Glencoe during these years. Their spirit and determination were admired by W H Murray, who observed they '*had a speed and confidence we simply hadn't possessed. After we had climbed the Garrick Shelf on the Buachaille our immediate feeling was one of "never again". These fellows were starting with climbs like that, taking them almost for granted.*'

This new confidence grew partly out of the physical fitness that wartime training in survival skills had created. Better equipment, including nylon ropes and moulded rubber-soled boots, also helped this generation to take climbing to new heights. Developments in the 1960s in man-made materials saw slings and ropes becoming stronger and safer, and the adaptation of industrial materials that had arisen in the wartime decades continued. The Glasgow shipyards supplied many industrial nuts which were used as chocks for rock climbing. Once threaded with rope, the nut was

Left: Arthur Russell and his son George camping in Glencoe during the 1930s. Arthur, a keen member of the Scottish Mountaineering Club, was Law Agent of The National Trust for Scotland in 1935, when Glencoe was put up for sale by Lord Strathcona. Russell successfully acquired Signal Rock, the Clachaig Inn and other land in the Glen on behalf of the Trust. George later followed in his father's footsteps as the Trust's Law Agent

Below: SC Gully, a classic gully climb in Stob Coire nan Lochan

jammed into a crack in the rock and the leader's rope clipped onto it with a karabiner. This simple device provided a running belay in the event of a fall and greatly increased the safety of many routes.

Developments in technology continued in the 1970s, enabling cutting-edge climbers to reach higher standards. An international interest in climbing and changes in attitudes towards the sport saw mountaineering in Glencoe take on a fresh lease of life in the 1970s and 80s. Many difficult first ascents were made by young climbers, often without the use of the climbing aids used by earlier generations. Fitness levels reached a new high and sport climbing became fashionable, although its use of pre-placed bolts drilled into the rock also made it controversial. Climbers like **Dave Cuthbertson** and **Murray Hamilton** led the way, making many bold and imaginative ascents, including Elliot's Downfall on Aonach Dubh and Frozen Ba's on the Etive Slabs. They were joined by others such as **Ken Johnston**, **Kenny McClusky** and **Pete Greenwell** from Glasgow and **Rab Anderson** and **Alan Taylor** from Edinburgh. Rab Anderson recalled his early introduction to Glencoe. *'Whilst still at school, we used to hitch up and camp in the shadow of the Buachaille at Jacksonville – the start of our long association with these rocks. Back then there were the great routes climbed by our heroes: Gallows Route, Shibboleth, Carnivore, Trapeze and others. Enough to strike fear into some hearts but they were the stuff that schoolboy dreams were made of. It was this that lured us to Glencoe.'*

The 1980s brought a radical leap in standards of performance as well as a shift in the perception of what was physically possible. Training programmes, previously the preserve of the elite, began to be embraced by the general climbing population. Climbing in Glencoe has continued to hold its place at the forefront of mountaineering sport with some of the hardest summer and winter routes in Britain. And it is this huge diversity of climbs which has made the area so pivotal in the history of Scottish mountaineering. As mountaineer Graeme Ettle says: *'There is a vast amount of new routes still to be climbed. Every decade that goes by sees new skills and techniques being developed, new gear, new attitudes and new inspirations for doing routes.'* Glencoe's future as a centre of mountaineering excellence is anything but rocky.

'Yet it is without doubt the most majestic and the most dramatic of all Scotland's glens – a rich mix of brooding history, glistening rock, soaring buttresses, and towering peaks, which are usually hidden from view under constantly shifting veils of mist.'

Roly Smith, *The Guardian*, 18 November 2000

Dave Cuthbertson on Bidean nam Bian.
Inset: climbing the 'Crocodile' on the east face of Aonach Dubh

043

Seven of the best hill routes in the Glencoe area. They cover all eight Munros on the NTS property – and three more nearby for Munro-baggers.

1 Buachaille Etive Mòr

Pronounced: booachil etiv moar
Means: The Big Herdsman of Etive
Height: 1,022 metres (3,350 ft)
Recognise it: This classic pyramidal mountain rises from the flat expanse of Rannoch Moor and guards the eastern approach to Glencoe. Its highest summit is Stob Dearg, which earns its name 'the red peak' from the coloured rhyolite that forms its jaggy peaks and crags. A second Munro, Stob na Bròige (Peak of the Shoe), lies at the south-west end of the ridge, overlooking Glen Etive.

2 Buachaille Etive Beag

Pronounced: booachil etiv bek
Means: Small Herdsman of Etive
Height: 958 metres (3,143 ft)
Recognise it: The big herdsman's little brother, Buachaille Etive Beag, shelters behind the larger, more imposing mountain. It has two Munros: Stob Coire Raineach (Peak of the Corrie of Ferns) and Stob Dubh (Black Peak), at either end of its ridge.

3 Bidean nam Bian

Pronounced: beetyan nam beeoan
Means: Point of the Hinds
Height: 1,150 metres (3,773 ft)
Recognise it: As its name suggests, Bidean nam Bian is the highest peak in Argyll and the highest point in a large and complex massif which comprises eight mountains, four great ridges and three main corries. It takes in The Three Sisters (Beinn Fhada, 'The Long Mountain'; Gearr Aonach, 'The Short Ridge'; and Aonach Dubh, 'The Black Ridge') which form an imposing flank to the south of the Glen, with their near-vertical cliffs and dark scree. Standing 1 km north-east of Bidean is its satellite summit Stob Coire nan Lochan, which rises to 1,115 metres.

4 Stob Coire Sgreamhach

Pronounced: stop korra skree-yach
Means: Peak of the Fearful Corrie
Height: 1,072 metres (3,517 ft)
Recognise it Part of the Bidean massif, this mountain reaches out to the first of The Three Sisters, Beinn Fhada. It was elevated to Munro status in 1998.

5 Sgor na h-Ulaidh

Pronounced: skor na hoolya
Means: Peak of the Buried Treasure
Height: 994 metres (3,261 ft)
Recognise it: Sometimes called the Lost Mountain of Glencoe, Sgor na h-Ulaidh lies west of the long ridge of Bidean nam Bian.

6 Beinn a' Bheithir

Pronounced: byn vair
Means: Hill of the Bear (though commonly known as Hill of the Thunderbolt)
Height: 1,024 metres (3,360 ft)
Recognise it: Lying to the west of Glencoe this large, impressive mountain overlooks the Ballachulish Bridge and comprises two Munros, Sgorr Dhearg (Red Peak) and Sgorr Dhonuill (Donald's Peak).

7 Aonach Eagach

Pronounced: oenoch egoch
Means: The Notched Ridge
Height: 967 metres (3,173 ft)
Recognise it: Dominating the north side of Glencoe, the Aonach Eagach ridge stretches 9 km from the Devil's Staircase in the east to the Pap of Glencoe in the west. Its highest peak is Sgorr nam Fiannaidh (The Peak of the Feinn or Giants), which rises to 967 metres (3,173 ft). To the east is the ridge's second Munro, Meall Dearg (Red Hill) at 953 metres (3,127 ft).

Respect the mountains

Mountaineering is, by its very nature, a potentially hazardous activity; routes can be difficult and weather often changes with little warning. You should set out only if you are properly equipped and have adequate experience for the route you are undertaking. Here are a few guidelines to help keep you safe and secure.

 Learn how to read a map and a compass

 Fill in a route card and leave it with someone who knows your time of return

 Plan your route in advance

 Be properly equipped

 Always carry a head-torch

 Check the local weather forecast

 Know your limits

 Start early, finish early

 Take sufficient food

 Carry a first aid kit

Main picture: looking towards The Three Sisters from An Bodach
Right: climbing on the Aonach Eagach ridge (top) and on 'Lady Jane', Aonach Dubh (bottom)

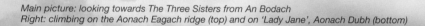

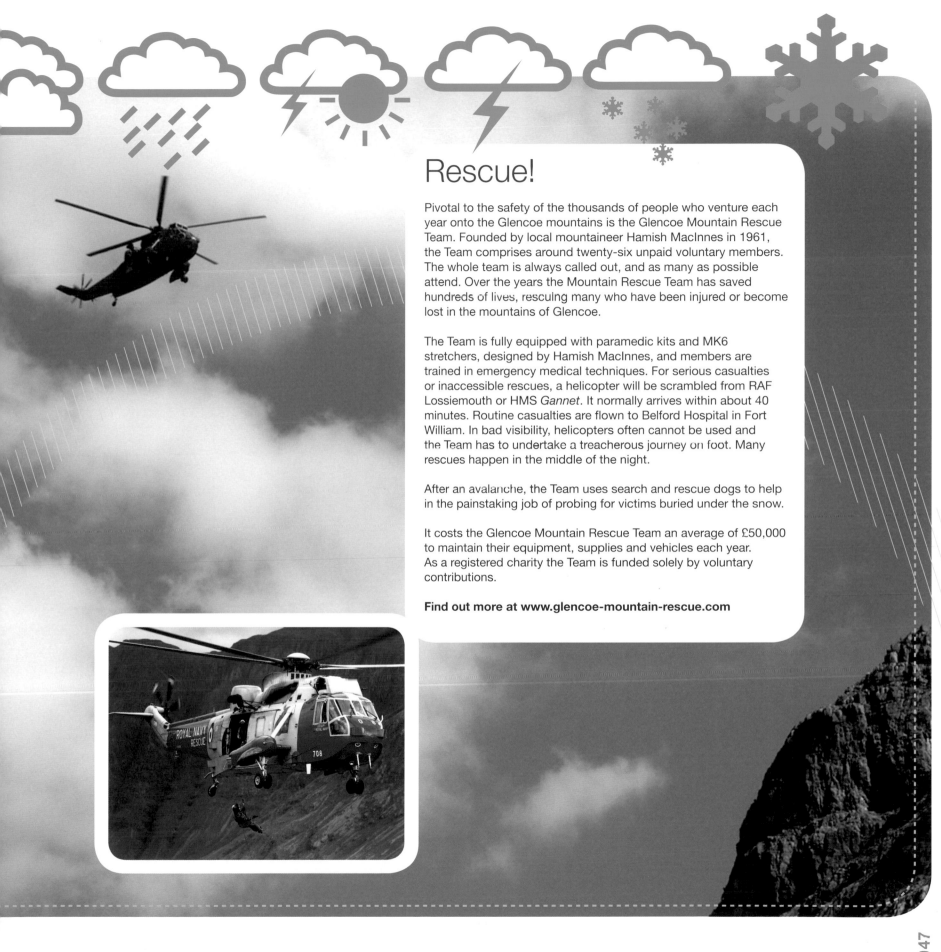

Rescue!

Pivotal to the safety of the thousands of people who venture each year onto the Glencoe mountains is the Glencoe Mountain Rescue Team. Founded by local mountaineer Hamish MacInnes in 1961, the Team comprises around twenty-six unpaid voluntary members. The whole team is always called out, and as many as possible attend. Over the years the Mountain Rescue Team has saved hundreds of lives, rescuing many who have been injured or become lost in the mountains of Glencoe.

The Team is fully equipped with paramedic kits and MK6 stretchers, designed by Hamish MacInnes, and members are trained in emergency medical techniques. For serious casualties or inaccessible rescues, a helicopter will be scrambled from RAF Lossiemouth or HMS *Gannet*. It normally arrives within about 40 minutes. Routine casualties are flown to Belford Hospital in Fort William. In bad visibility, helicopters often cannot be used and the Team has to undertake a treacherous journey on foot. Many rescues happen in the middle of the night.

After an avalanche, the Team uses search and rescue dogs to help in the painstaking job of probing for victims buried under the snow.

It costs the Glencoe Mountain Rescue Team an average of £50,000 to maintain their equipment, supplies and vehicles each year. As a registered charity the Team is funded solely by voluntary contributions.

Find out more at www.glencoe-mountain-rescue.com

Glencoe:
witness to dramatic history

'Go to any place where history
is stored and listen. Hold your
breath. Hear how still it is.'

A L Kennedy, 1990

Alexander Nasmyth (1758-1840): Glencoe

More than 300 years after the event, Glencoe's name remains synonymous with the brutal slaughter that occurred there in the early hours of 13 February 1692. Thirty-eight men, women and children, all MacDonalds, were murdered in cold blood by troops carrying out government orders. Others died trying to escape into the freezing winter mountains. Public shock at the Massacre of Glencoe reverberated throughout the country.

For many Glencoe will always be associated with the MacDonalds, but the area's history stretches back long before the name of this clan became associated with the area. While no firm evidence survives of the very first settlers in the Glen, the shores of Loch Leven would have provided plentiful resources for hunter-gatherers some 6,000 to 8,000 years ago. Between 4,000 and 6,000 years ago, more established farming settlements would have developed along the shores and in the glens. More recent land uses have either destroyed or covered over the remains associated with these prehistoric and early historic peoples of Glencoe. But there is every reason to expect that these are awaiting discovery: in 1880 such a find was made when workers digging in the Ballachulish Moss on the north side of Loch Leven turned up a large carved wooden female figure, encased in wickerwork, which had been there for over 2,500 years. It is associated with Iron Age ritual and belief.

Right: this ancient wooden figure, found in the Ballachulish Moss, is now in the Museum of Scotland in Edinburgh, as are the amber beads, below, used by the MacDonalds as a charm against blindness

John Knox (1778-1845): Glencoe

'Glencoe is described as one of the most interesting scenes in the whole country; hung with rock, and wood; and abounding with beauties of the most romantic kind.'

William Gilpin, *Observations ... particularly [on] the Highlands of Scotland ... made in the year 1776*, published 1808

'All the way, the road had been among moors and mountains with huge masses of rock, which fell down God knows where, sprinkling the ground in every direction, and giving it the aspect of the burial place of a race of giants. Now and then we passed a hut or two, with neither window nor chimney, and the smoke of the peat fire rolling out at the door. But there were not six of these dwellings in a dozen miles; and anything so bleak and wild, and mighty in its loneliness, as the whole country, it is impossible to conceive.'

Charles Dickens, *Letters*, 1841

Background: 1746 map of General Wade's military roads in the Highlands, showing 'Glen Coen'

Above: Eilean Munde

Below: an engraving of 1842 showing a West Highland cow and young bull

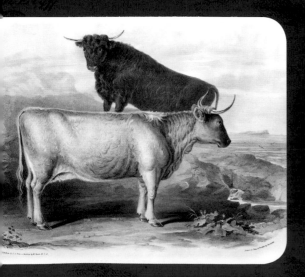

Pagan rites continued in the area for well over a thousand years before Christianity was adopted. The oldest known Christian site in the area is on Eilean Munde in Loch Leven, dedicated to St Fintan Mundus, a sixth-century missionary. Today, remains of an ancient chapel and burial ground can still be seen. In later centuries the Stewarts of Ballachulish, the Camerons of Onich and the MacDonalds of Glencoe were also buried here.

The earliest historic records about Glencoe date from the late thirteenth and early fourteenth centuries, the period of the Wars of Independence, when Scottish nobles were struggling to free themselves from English domination. The MacDougalls – who owned the land at that time – found themselves on the wrong side of King Robert the Bruce. Their lands were divided up and given to the king's allies and supporters. One of the first in line was Angus Og, who had brought the MacDonalds to fight for the king at Bannockburn. In turn, Angus passed the lands of Glencoe to his son Iain og Fhraoch (Iain of the Heather), and his ownership of the '*terram de Glanchomyr*' is confirmed in a medieval charter of 1343. His descendants took his title and were known as the MacIain MacDonalds.

Unfortunately for the MacIains, by the second half of the fifteenth century the power of the MacDonald Lords of the Isles was beginning to crumble. In 1493 James IV – aided by the first Earl of Argyll, Colin Campbell – finally succeeded in abolishing the Lordship. Among the possessions seized by the Crown were the lands of Glencoe. The MacIain MacDonalds who lived in the Glen had no charter or legal title to their lands, holding them only 'by the sword'. So they now became tenants under a series of different clan chiefs – first the Stewarts of Appin and then the Campbells of Glenorchy and Argyll.

At its peak the MacIain MacDonald clan numbered between 500 and 600 people, living in an area that stretched along the southern shores of Loch Leven from west of Ballachulish to east of Invercoe and south along Glen Coe. In the late seventeenth century the lands were described in glowing terms by the cartographer and antiquarian Robert Gordon:

'This Glencone is a twenty markland, which pertaineth to certane of the Clandonald. This countrie is verie profitable fertill and plenteous of corne, milk, butter, cheese and abundance of fish both salmond and herrings and other kynd of fishes therein.'

In the seventeenth century sturdy black cattle were raised and grazed here, sheep were kept for their wool, milk and meat, and barley and oats were grown. Houses were traditionally built of stone, turf and wattle and thatched with straw, bracken or heather. The climate was harsh and life may often have been a struggle, but the MacIain MacDonalds of Glencoe were a fiercely proud and independent people.

Much has been made of the clan rivalry between the MacDonalds and the Campbells during the seventeenth century. The MacDonalds did raid cattle from their Campbell neighbours, but so did many clans: the activity was common throughout the Highlands, since cattle were among the most valuable commodities. Further tensions arose between the clans when Archibald Campbell, the 10th Earl of Argyll, gained unrivalled power and influence in his unofficial role as the King's agent in the Highlands. Politically, too, the MacDonalds and the Campbells held opposing views. The Campbells were supporters of the Protestant King William of Orange, who had gained the thrones of England and Scotland when the Catholic King James VII fled to France in 1689. In contrast, the MacDonalds were Jacobites, supporters of James, whom they believed to be the rightful King. The Massacre of Glencoe has often been portrayed as a tale of Campbells butchering MacDonalds, but in reality responsibility for the Massacre went right to the heart of the establishment: it was part of a government plan to bring the troublesome Highlanders into line behind King William.

James VII of Scotland and II of England, by an unknown artist, c1690

In London in the late 1680s there was real concern about the possible Jacobite threat to restore James to the throne. MacIain of Glencoe was one of many Highland chiefs who had fought for the Jacobite cause at the Battle of Killiecrankie in 1689. The government decided to respond to the threat by announcing, on 27 August 1691, an Indemnity, stating that all Jacobite chiefs who swore the oath of allegiance to William and Mary would be free from penalties for previous crimes and would receive the protection of the Crown. Those who refused would be punished by the utmost extremity of the law as traitors and rebels. A deadline of 1 January 1692 was set for the clan chiefs to take the oath.

Administering the policy was the King's Secretary of State for Scotland, John Dalrymple, Master of Stair. Described as being harsh in language and capable of a brand of invective that won him few close friends, Stair had little time for the Highlanders, whom he regarded, from his panelled offices in London's Kensington Palace, as savages. By mid-December, Stair was already planning a campaign should any chief fail to take the oath, and on 29 December 1691, on Stair's orders, 800 men from the Earl of Argyll's regiment advanced north from Inveraray. Meanwhile the Highland chiefs were still awaiting word from the exiled King James, for no chief was prepared to sign an oath without his jurisdiction. As soon as the Indemnity had been announced in August, two messengers had set off secretly for France to bring back word from the King. But James had dithered, only giving his word on 12 December and wasting much precious time. It is not known when word finally reached MacIain in Glencoe: it may have been on 29 December, two days before the deadline expired. For it was then, in heavy snows, that MacIain set out to take the oath, making the fatal mistake of travelling to Fort William instead of Inveraray.

William of Orange, later William III, after Sir Peter Lely, 1677

Arriving late that day to give his oath to Colonel Hill, the Governor at Fort William, MacIain learned of his error. It must have been with heavy hearts that he and his men set out again into the driving snow, this time heading for Inveraray, some 60 miles away. Further misfortune struck when they were detained en route by government troops for twenty-four hours. All hope of reaching Inveraray on time was now lost. Struggling on, MacIain finally arrived on 3 January 1692, two days after the deadline had expired. After much pleading with the local sheriff, he was allowed to take the oath of allegiance to King William on 6 January and left Inveraray believing that his clan was safe. But unbeknown to him, the Privy Council in Edinburgh discounted his oath and removed his name from the list. Glencoe's fate was sealed.

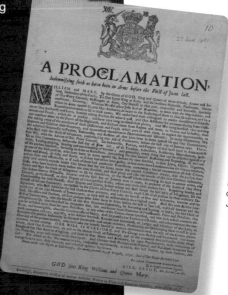

Royal indemnity of 1691 for Jacobite chiefs

By fire and sword

On 11 January 1692, John Dalrymple, Master of Stair, issued instructions to Sir Thomas Livingstone, the commander-in-chief of the King's forces in Scotland:

> *'You are hereby ordered & authorised to march our Troops which are now posted at Inverlochy & Invernes, to act against these Highland Rebells who has not taken the benefite of our Indemnity, by fire & sword, and all manner of Hostility to burne their houses, seise or destroy their goods or Cattell, plenishing or Cloaths and to cut off the men.'*

Six days later Sir Thomas Livingstone transmitted Stair's orders further down the line to Colonel Hill, commander of the garrison at Fort William. But Hill, more sympathetic to the Highlanders, distanced himself from the proceedings. So it was to his deputy, Lieutenant Colonel Hamilton, that final orders were sent. On 23 January, Sir Thomas Livingstone wrote to Hamilton:

> *'I understand the Laird of Glenco coming aftir the prefixt time, was not admitted to take the oath, which is very good news to Us here …Colonell, I desir you may begin with Glenco – and spare nothing that belongs to him, And do not trouble the Government with Prisoners.'*

And it was Hamilton who issued the crucial instructions as to how Glencoe was to be taken.

Some 400 soldiers of the Earl of Argyll's regiment, under the command of Major Robert Duncanson, were stationed at Ballachulish. On 1 February, 120 redcoat soldiers marched out of Ballachulish accompanied by Captain Robert Campbell of Glenlyon. Later that day they arrived at Glencoe with a letter from Colonel Hill instructing the villagers to provide bed and board for the troops. Although it was a Highland tradition to offer such hospitality, in reality Maclain and his clan had little choice but to permit the soldiers to stay. He may have believed that this was a test of his loyalty; it is fairly certain that he did not know that his oath had been discounted. For twelve days the troops slept in the villagers' cramped houses, took meals with them, shared whisky and wine, and told stories around the fire.

It is unlikely that the soldiers were aware of the true purpose of their stay. But behind the scenes, the final details were being put into place. On 30 January, Stair penned his last letter to Colonel Hill: *'When any thing concerning Glencoe is resolved lett it be secret & sudden … '* It was on 12 February 1692 that the now infamous order was passed to the last in the chain of command, Captain Robert Campbell of Glenlyon, who was to attack Glencoe at 5 o'clock in the morning. The order from Major Duncanson read:

> *'You are hereby ordered to fall upon the Rebells, the McDonalds of Glenco, and putt all to the sword under Seventy, you are to have a Speciall care that the old ffox and his Sones doe upon no account escape your hands. You are to secure all the avenues thatt no man escape. This you are to putt in executione att fyve of the clock precisely…This is by the Kings Speciall command.'*

Sir Thomas Livingstone's letter to Lieutenant Colonel Hamilton ordering the Massacre

John Dalrymple, Master of Stair, by Sir John de Medina

Captain Robert Campbell of Glenlyon, by an unknown artist

You are hereby ordered to fall upon the Rebells, the McDonalds of Glenco, and putt all to the sword under seventy. you are to have a speciall care that the old Fox and his sones doe upon no account escape your hands, you are to secure all the avenues that no man escape. this you are to putt in execution att fyve of the clock precisely; and by that time or verie shortly after it, I'le strive to be att you with a stronger party: if I doe not come to you att fyve, you are not to tary for me, butt to fall on. This is by the Kings speciall command, for the good & safty of the Country, that these miscreants be cutt off root and branch. See that this be putt in execution without feud or favour, else you may expect to be dealt with as one not true to King nor Government, nor a man fitt to carry Commissione in the Kings service. Expecting you will not faill in the fulfilling hereof, as you love your selfe, I subscribe these with my hand att Balichdis Feb: 12, 1692

For their Maties service.

To Capt
Robert Campbell
of Glenlyon.

The order to Captain Campbell from Major Duncanson to 'fall upon the Rebells, the McDonalds of Glenco'

David Young Cameron: Shadows of Glencoe, 1925

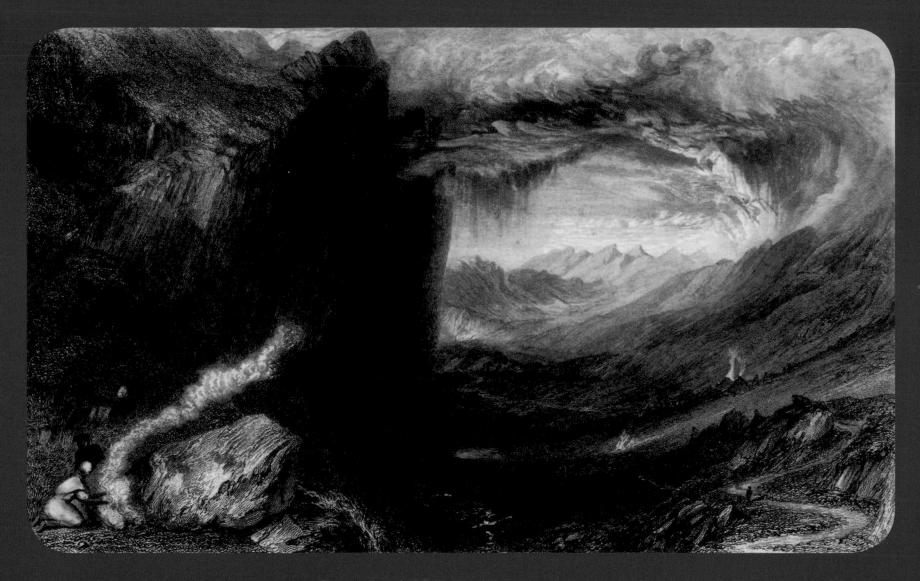

Above: Glencoe, 1834-6: intaglio print after J M W Turner, from Walter Scott's Prose Works

Opposite page, top: J Merigot, View in Glencoe, 1801

Bottom left: warrant issued by William III for a Commission of Inquiry into the Massacre, April 1695

Bottom right: monument in Glencoe village to the MacDonalds killed in the Massacre

The morning of 13 February 1692 was freezing cold, with an icy wind bringing snowstorms down from the mountains. Shortly before 5 am, Glenlyon summoned his men to give them their orders. At 5 o'clock precisely Glenlyon's lieutenant knocked on the door of the clan chief's house. Moments later Maclain lay dead, a bullet in his back. It is difficult to comprehend the fear and terror that must have been felt as the clan realised what was happening. It was a horrific event with thirty-eight recorded murders. Accounts tell of a young boy begging for his life, only to be shot; of nine men tied together and executed. Many more died of exposure, evading the initial onslaught but falling victim to the harsh weather in the mountains. But others did escape. Maclain's sons John and Alasdair survived, together with most of the clan. Perhaps the bad weather hampered the attack, or many of the MacDonalds fled on hearing the first shots. Maybe the soldiers themselves were unwilling to carry out the appalling task of slaughtering their hosts; there are certainly many unconfirmed stories of soldiers passing on warnings. The government orders had called for total annihilation and Stair's response to Colonel Hill on 5 March stated his only regret:

> *'The affair of Glencoe is much talked of here … all I regrate is that any of that sort gott away and there is necessity to prosecute them to the utmost.'*

As news of the Massacre filtered through slowly to London, there was genuine shock. It was the breach of hospitality that made the killings stand out as an atrocity. A letter written to the Countess of Melville on 8 March 1692 summed up some of the public feeling, *'It is reputed one of the most barbarous things that has been done in this countrey; Glen Lyon affirms that the first person he killed was the landlord he had lodged with 3 days befor …'*

The Jacobites were instrumental in bringing the details of the Massacre to the public's attention. In April 1692 a description of the event was printed in the French *Paris Gazette* and the following year a pamphlet was published in London. In an effort to appease parliament and salvage the government's reputation, a brief parliamentary inquiry was set up in 1693 but it progressed slowly and its findings were not pursued. Three years later another inquiry was commissioned. Livingstone and Hill were cleared of any responsibility; Hamilton, Duncanson and Glenlyon were recommended for prosecution but they were never brought to trial. The King was absolved of any wrongdoing. The bulk of the blame was laid with John Dalrymple, the Master of Stair, who '*had exceeded your Majesties Instructions towards the killing and destruction of the Glencoemen*'. Stair clung on to office until 1695 when he resigned as Secretary of State, but it was not the end of his political career and in later years he was created 2nd Viscount and 1st Earl of Stair.

In the weeks that followed the Massacre, the MacDonalds sought refuge with their neighbouring clansmen, who fed and harboured them. Colonel Hill urged the Privy Council to pardon the survivors and let them return to the Glen. But it took until August before he was able to issue a proclamation offering them royal protection in return for taking an oath of allegiance. Only then could John MacDonald, now the thirteenth chief of Glencoe, swear the same oath that his father had taken eight months previously in Inveraray, and bring his people home.

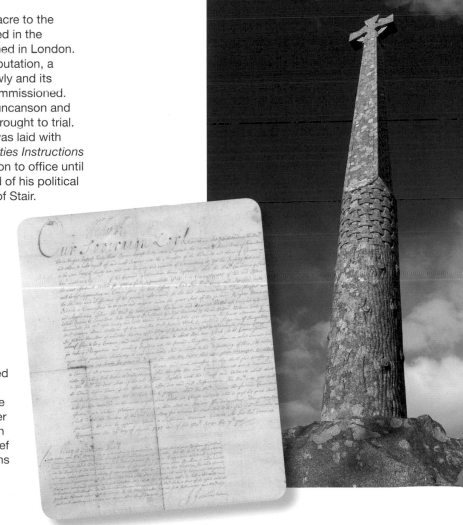

Gradually the MacDonalds of Glencoe rebuilt their homes and picked up the threads of their old life. Their support for the Jacobite cause did not dwindle. In 1745 the MacDonalds of Glencoe backed Bonnie Prince Charlie in his fight to reclaim the throne for his father and over 100 men of Glencoe fought for the cause at the Battle of Culloden in 1746. In the months after Culloden, the early submission by the Chief to the government probably saved his clan from summary executions and the wasting of their land.

The sword in the water

Local amateur historian Arthur Smith who, sadly, died in 2005, was brought up in the 1930s by his Gaelic-speaking grandmother. In a time of no television and limited radio, she would entertain him with marvellous stories of the Jacobites and the myths and legends of the Glen. Here he recounts the strange story of Corrag the Witch.

'One of the stories told to me by my Granny was of a local witch, Corrag. At the time of the Massacre, Corrag had warned everybody that the Redcoats were up to no good, but nobody listened. The evening before the Massacre, Corrag fled up into the hills, wrapped herself in a plaid and stayed out all night. She came back the next day and the village was empty, the houses were burned, the cattle had been driven off and there was just the haze of smoke lying over the Glen. The myth is that she went to where Maclain, the Chief, had been shot by the Redcoats and she took his broadsword down the Glen to the Narrows, where she threw the sword into the water. Corrag made a prophecy that the men of the Glen had suffered enough, and as long as that sword lay undisturbed by the hand of man, no man from this Glen would ever die by the sword again. Now that's the myth and the legend.

I have checked, nobody from Glencoe was killed at Culloden, nobody was killed at Waterloo or the Thin Red Line, Balaclava, and nobody from the village was killed in any of the Victorian wars. During the Boer War in 1900, the boy McCall died but that was cholera and Granny said that didn't count. 1914, 1915, 1916 nobody from the village was killed and then in June 1916, they brought up a dredger from Glasgow to dredge the loch to get bigger ships in and out for the smelter at Kinlochleven, for the war effort. On the night of 30 June 1916, the captain of the dredger went into the Old Glen Hotel with a handle of an old sword that had come up in the basket. The men were horrified and rode out into the loch and threw it back in. Now that is fact. And the other fact was that next morning, seven men from the village were killed at the Western Front and up until then nobody. Now you can mix fact and legend or it could be a coincidence – 1 July 1916 was the first Battle of the Somme and the casualties were enormous.'

Hugh William Williams (1773-1829): Glencoe

In 1769 there were still six farms in the Glen where sheep and black cattle were kept for milk, butter and cheese and the ground worked in traditional strips with crops of barley and oats. Hunting, fishing and gathering shellfish, seaweed and wild plants for food and medicine were all part of daily life. But at about this time the area around Glencoe and Appin, in common with most of the Highlands, witnessed social and demographic upheaval as economic changes took place. Many families were evicted from their land to make way for more efficient sheep rearing, in the century-long turmoil known as the Clearances. Commenting in the early 1800s, one visitor to Glencoe remarked: *'The sheep-farming system has done the work of extirpation more effectively than the ... Massacre.'* Large numbers of people set sail for a new life in North America. Others started work at the newly opened slate quarries at Ballachulish, an industry that grew so dramatically that by 1781 seventy-four families were based there. By 1845, the workforce had almost doubled to 587 men, who in a single year produced 26 million slates. Despite these social changes, Gaelic remained the language of many: in 1891 of the 1,480 people living in Glencoe and Ballachulish, all but 250 were Gaelic speakers.

One of those who chose a new life outside the Glen was the seventeenth Clan Chief, Ewen MacDonald. He moved to India to practise as a doctor. When he died, in 1837, the lands of Glencoe passed to his daughter and she in turn sold Glencoe to Lord Strathcona who made his name with the Canadian Hudson Bay Company. In 1935 Lord Strathcona sold the lands of Glencoe, some of which were purchased by The National Trust for Scotland to safeguard them for the nation. Later, the Scottish Mountaineering Club bought Dalness Estate from the last MacDonalds of Dalness, and gave it to the Trust.

Above: sheep farm in Glencoe c1930

What the Glen means to me

We asked some of the local schoolchildren at Glencoe Primary School what the Glen means to them. The school is in Glencoe village, and has 42 pupils, taught in two classes. These are a selection of the entries.

'Glencoe is an amazing place to live in because of the hills, the fresh air, the space, the views of the Glen and the exercise you get as you explore the whole area all year round. My only dislike in Glencoe is that it is usually raining (apart from the summer) which is a bit annoying when you have everything you want on your doorstep.'

Robbie Nelson, age 11

'Glencoe is a wonderful place to live. There are mountains surrounding the village, and as I walk home from school I see the Pap of Glencoe looking down at me. Summer is my favourite time of year because after school I get ready to head off to the Tidal pool or the Clachaig pool. I love going in the cool refreshing rivers. It's so much fun trying to swim up the rapids and jumping off the high rocks.'

Jessica Stewart, age 12

'Wherever you go in the Glen, you see mountains and the most attractive mountain is the Pap of Glencoe because it has a lot of history like the Massacre of Glencoe. It started and finished in February 1692 and to this day people are still remembering the people who died. There was a monument made in Glencoe in 1884 by Mrs Burns MacDonald so that the memory will last for evermore. Every year our school takes part in the anniversary. I really appreciate being brought up in Glencoe because of the wonderful environment and healthy children and adults.'

Marc MacLachlan, age 12

'I have lived in Glencoe all my life and have never once wanted to live anywhere else! Why would I want to live anywhere else? I live in Glencoe village – a small, mysterious village nestled at the foot of the Pap of Glencoe, a beautiful and majestic mountain. Further up the Glen the scenery becomes more rugged, the mountains get higher, the rivers get stronger and wider. The mountains become entangled by a cloak of rough, purple heather and twisted bracken. Also more wildlife begins to appear in the air and on the land. I can't imagine living anywhere else but Glencoe. Do you want to know what the Glen means to me? EVERYTHING!'

Lucy Doogan, age 11

Anti-clockwise from top left: trimming slates at the Ballachulish slate quarry in the 1950s; a milkmaid in Ballachulish during the 1920s or 1930s; houses in Glencoe c1880; pupils at Glencoe village school, c1900, and their modern counterparts learning about local wildlife with a Ranger

Glencoe:
the great outdoors

'It does have majesty of the wildest kind. The eye lifts from glen to rock peaks packed in close array, trenched by ravines and towering bluntly. Of its kind it is unrivalled. Most other glens become tame by comparison ...'

W H Murray, 1962

GLENCOE
Visitor Centre

A green building

In May 2002, The National Trust for Scotland opened its new award-winning Visitor Centre at Inverigan, close to Glencoe village. A visitor centre had been constructed in the middle glen opposite the Clachaig in 1976 by the Countryside Commission for Scotland, as an early experiment in visitor management. It was designed to replace the unsightly vending then going on throughout the glen: in this it was highly successful and ultimately it could not cope with the visitor numbers it attracted. Its location had also been controversial and the decision to move to the lower glen, amongst screening trees, was widely welcomed. The 1976 building was demolished in 2002.

The new Visitor Centre has been constructed along the very best ecological guidelines. Situated back from the main road, the Centre's low-roofed buildings are designed around the concept of a clachan, a traditional Highland village. The buildings sit amidst a birch wood and are raised on stilts to ensure that the trees' roots are undisturbed. Water for the Centre is collected and filtered on site, and waste water is treated and recycled into the River Coe as pure water. The buildings are constructed from Scottish timber with slate and corrugated iron roofs. The energy efficiency of the Visitor Centre has been maximised using recycled paper insulation in the walls and sheep's wool, in place of foam, to insulate around the windows. An environmentally-friendly woodchip boiler provides heating for the Centre.

This secluded complex harmonises perfectly with its surroundings, yet it also allows us to cater efficiently for the 180,000 visitors who visit the Centre each year to enjoy its superb facilities. An exciting interactive exhibition allows visitors to explore the area and discover its fascinating history, ecology and geology. There is lots for children to do too, with a quest to solve and interactive games and puzzles. A café, a viewing platform offering panoramic views of the Glen, a well-stocked shop and an education suite all add to the Centre's appeal. The Glencoe Ranger Service runs a programme of events and activities including the popular Land Rover Wildlife Safaris.

WATCH YOUR STEP!

Keeping to paths ensures that plants are protected from being trampled and reduces damage to the landscape.

Stones and rocks are homes for all kinds of lichen, insects and small creatures, so don't be tempted to build cairns.

Mountain bikes create soil erosion and damage plants.

Walk 2

Peninsula Walk

Just 2 miles from Glencoe, Ballachulish lies on the south side of Loch Leven. It became famous because of the slate quarries which operated for over 250 years until 1955. It is still possible to see the disused quarries at the eastern end of Ballachulish.

This is a circular route along a grassy path, on land reclaimed from the slate quarry. From the car park you can see some of the old boat sheds built of slate.

This walk can often be wet underfoot, so waterproof walking shoes are advised. The path is accessible for wheelchairs.

How long
1 mile (1.5 km) walk, allow 1 hour round trip.

How to get there
Start from the car park at the old quarry harbour by the Isles of Glencoe Hotel in the village of Ballachulish, 2 miles north of the Visitor Centre, along the A82. You can also walk around the quarry itself, located behind the Tourist Information Centre at Ballachulish.

What to look for
The quarry was opened at the end of the 1600s and at its height in the late 1800s it employed nearly 600 people, producing slate which was shipped as far afield as America. Most of the slates were used for roofing and for pavements. It was the tradition that when a man retired from working at the quarry, he was given a slab of slate to make his own headstone, many of which are very beautifully and intricately carved.

This walk gives superb views over Loch Leven to Eilean Munde, the burial isle. Believed to have been home to St Fintan Mundus, a sixth-century missionary, it became an important local religious site. The remains of a church built in the 1500s can still be seen, together with the graves of several generations of local people, including Maclain of Glencoe, the MacDonald chief killed during the Massacre. Next to Eilean Munde lies the smaller island Eilean a' Chomhraidh, or the Isle of Discussion, where local disputes were traditionally settled.

Linking South Ballachulish to North Ballachulish across Loch Leven is the modern steel Ballachulish Bridge which opened in 1975. Before that a ferry operated, and you can still see the slipways that served the ferries on either side of the loch.

Level: Easy

Walks 3, 4 & 5

Lochan Trails

There are three walks of differing length around the lochan lying directly north of Glencoe village. This area was originally owned by Lord Strathcona, who rose to fame with the Hudson Bay Company and became a partner in the Canadian Pacific Railway. He built the house which is now Glencoe Hospital, and created the lochan surrounded by conifer and maple trees in the late 1800s for his homesick native American wife. Lord Strathcona owned the whole estate of Glencoe until 1935 when part of it was bought by The National Trust for Scotland to safeguard its future.

How long

1-3 hours depending on whether you take one or all of the routes. *There is wheelchair access on the route which leads round the lochan.*

How to get there

Start from the car park, signposted on the road to Glencoe Hospital. The road is at the eastern end of Glencoe village main street.

What to look for

This area is owned by Forestry Commission Scotland and is well signposted. Interpretation panels provide information on wildlife and history and there is a viewpoint on the way up from the village before you reach the hospital. Rhododendron 'jungles' feature along the walk and overgrown islets can be seen dotting the lochan as well as a boathouse across the 'dam'. On the west side of the water there is a lily-pond framed by an arch formed from two intertwining rowan trees, a symbol of good luck.

Level: Easy

Further information from Lorne Forest District (T 01631 566155) or www.forestry.gov.uk/scotland

Walk 6

Mamore Lodge and Kinlochleven

A circular walk that follows part of the West Highland Way above the village of Kinlochleven, 7 miles (12 km) north-east of Glencoe. Kinlochleven nestles at the eastern end of the beautiful sea loch, Loch Leven. The walk is steep in places, but gives good views over the loch and the surrounding hills.

How long

Starting from Kinlochleven village, the walk is 3.75 miles (6 km) and you should allow two hours. If you are setting out on foot from Glencoe Visitor Centre it will add another 7 miles (12 km) to the walk.

How to get there

From the Glencoe Visitor Centre take the A82 to Glencoe village. Once you reach the village follow the B863 to Kinlochleven. The main walk starts from the car park next to St Paul's Church in Kinlochleven.

From the car park next to St Paul's Church take the path leading to the waterfall viewpoint. Turn right along the riverbank and follow the path up the hill and along to Mamore Lodge car park. You will then join the West Highland Way for a short distance, before arriving at Kinlochleven High School. From here cross the bridge which brings you back to the car park.

What to look for

Kinlochleven grew up in the early 1900s when an aluminium smelter was founded here, powered by hydro-electricity harnessed from the Blackwater Reservoir. You can still see the pipeline that brought water from the reservoir to the smelter until it closed in 2000. Today the Aluminium Story is told in Kinlochleven Visitor Centre. Hotels, cafés and shops can all be found in the village. There are great views too, especially over Loch Leven and the impressive Grey Mare's Tail waterfall.

Level: Medium

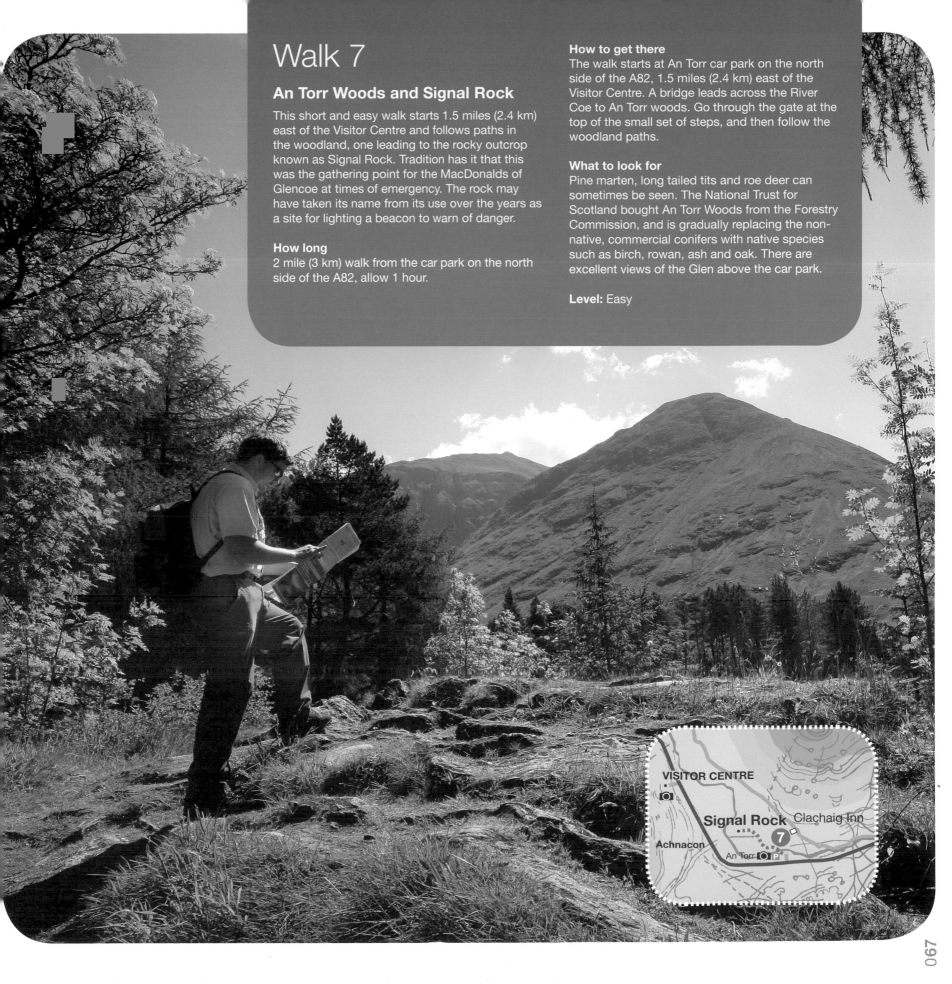

Walk 7

An Torr Woods and Signal Rock

This short and easy walk starts 1.5 miles (2.4 km) east of the Visitor Centre and follows paths in the woodland, one leading to the rocky outcrop known as Signal Rock. Tradition has it that this was the gathering point for the MacDonalds of Glencoe at times of emergency. The rock may have taken its name from its use over the years as a site for lighting a beacon to warn of danger.

How long

2 mile (3 km) walk from the car park on the north side of the A82, allow 1 hour.

How to get there

The walk starts at An Torr car park on the north side of the A82, 1.5 miles (2.4 km) east of the Visitor Centre. A bridge leads across the River Coe to An Torr woods. Go through the gate at the top of the small set of steps, and then follow the woodland paths.

What to look for

Pine marten, long tailed tits and roe deer can sometimes be seen. The National Trust for Scotland bought An Torr Woods from the Forestry Commission, and is gradually replacing the non-native, commercial conifers with native species such as birch, rowan, ash and oak. There are excellent views of the Glen above the car park.

Level: Easy

VISITOR CENTRE

Signal Rock   Clachaig Inn

Achnacon   7

An Torr   P

Walk 8

The West Highland Way

Part of the West Highland Way passes close to Glencoe. The 95 mile (152 km) walking route runs from Milngavie in Glasgow to Fort William along old shepherding paths, military roads and coaching routes.

From Kingshouse in the east to Kinlochleven in the north, the route follows the old military road built in the 1750s. From Kinlochleven the route continues north to Fort William, passing through spectacular scenery. The West Highland Way is a way-marked route and is intended for walkers. A good starting point is the car park at Altnafeadh.

Don't forget

Be properly equipped before you set out. Wear proper footwear and take waterproofs, as the weather can change quickly. Although this is a way-marked route, you should be able to read a map and compass to help with navigation if required.

Find out more at www.west-highland-way.co.uk

What to look for

Fantastic views towards Ben Nevis in the north-west as you reach the top of the Devil's Staircase and over the Glen to the south. Keep a look out for red deer that roam here.

Level: Medium

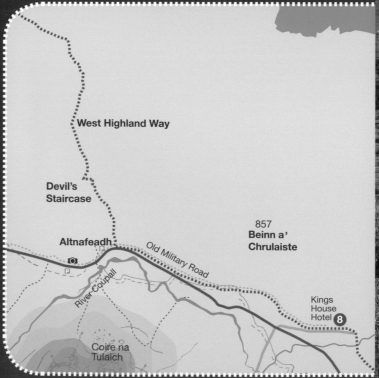

West Highland Way

Devil's Staircase

Altnafeadh

Old Military Road

857
Beinn a'
Chrulaiste

River Coupall

Kings House Hotel 8

Coire na Tulaich

BUACHAILLE ETIVE MÒR

One for the album

Glencoe is one of the most impressive and dramatic landscapes in Britain. Here are some great places to go in search of the perfect picture.

① Glencoe Visitor Centre Viewing Platform
Grid Ref: NN 112577
Fantastic views of Aonach Eagach in the east through to Meall Mòr in the west.

③ Achnambeithach Bridge
Grid Ref: NN 139568
Great for views of the ring fault at An t-Sron Gully, Loch Achtriochtan and Achnambeithach cottage with the coire behind.

⑤ Coire Gabhail Car Park
Grid Ref: NN 172568
A view further along the Glen of The Three Sisters. From here you can also view a 360° panorama of the Glen.

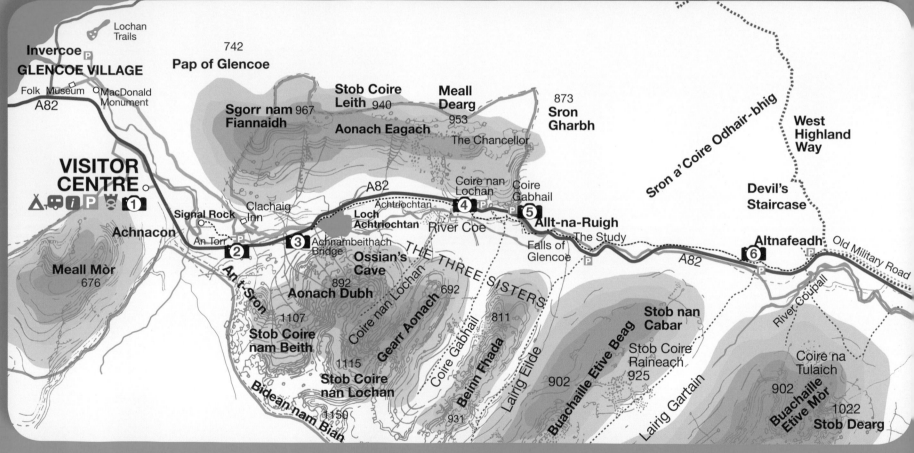

② An Torr Car Park
Grid Ref: NN 127564
This was the site of the old National Trust for Scotland Visitor Centre which has been knocked down and the landscape reinstated. From here there are 360° views which take in the Clachaig Gully and the Aonach Eagach ridge to the north, the Glen to the east, the mountains of Aonach Dubh and An t-Sron to the south and Meall Mòr to the west.

④ Coire nan Lochan Car Park
Grid Ref: NN 168569
From the car park there are excellent views of The Three Sisters and up the steep valley of Coire nan Lochan.

⑥ Car Park at Lairig Gartain (north end)
Grid Ref: NN 213559
Fantastic for a 360° view of the Glen, taking in Buachaille Etive Mòr and Buachaille Etive Beag to the south, Aonach Eagach, Sron a' Coire Odhair-bhig, the Devil's Staircase on the old military road to the north and Beinn a' Chrulaiste and Rannoch Moor to the east. Looking east between Beinn a' Chrulaiste and Buachaille Etive Mòr is an almost-perfect U-shaped valley.

References are from the Ordnance Survey Landranger 41 Ben Nevis, Fort William & Glen Coe map.

While you are in the area …

The National Trust for Scotland owns a number of other properties within easy driving distance of Glencoe that are well worth visiting.

Ben Lawers National Nature Reserve
Near Killin
The central Highlands' highest mountain, Ben Lawers rewards climbers and walkers with magnificent views. Enjoy the Trust's informative Visitor Centre and nature trails.
Tel 0844 493 2135

Glenfinnan Monument
Set in beautiful Highland scenery at the head of Loch Shiel, this inspiring monument pays tribute to the clansmen who joined Bonnie Prince Charlie here in 1745. An exhibition in the Visitor Centre tells the story of the ill-fated Jacobite campaign.
Tel 0844 493 2221

Killiecrankie
Near Pitlochry, Perthshire
Another site with Jacobite associations, this dramatic gorge witnessed the defeat of the government army by the rebels in 1689. The landscape here is rich in wildlife and interpretation in the Visitor Centre features the remarkable natural history as well as the famous battle.
Tel 0844 493 2194

Kintail & Morvich
A magnificent stretch of West Highland scenery. Within the Trust property are the spectacular Falls of Glomach, the Five Sisters of Kintail mountain range and the site of the battle of Glenshiel (1719).
Tel 0844 493 2230

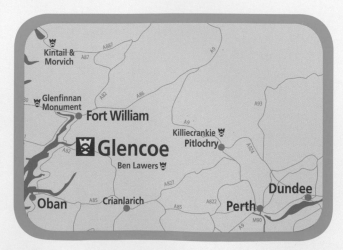

Access for all

The National Trust for Scotland welcomes disabled visitors to its properties. The following facilities are available at Glencoe:

- Designated spaces in car park for disabled visitors
- Visitor Centre, café and shop accessible
- Induction loops in Visitor Centre for visitors with a hearing impairment
- Handling items in Visitor Centre for visitors with a visual impairment
- Accessible toilets in Visitor Centre

The National Trust for Scotland

28 Charlotte Square, Edinburgh EH2 4ET
www.nts.org.uk
Scottish Charity No. SC 007410

The National Trust for Scotland is Scotland's leading conservation organisation. It is not a government department, but a charity supported by its membership of over 300,000.

The Trust was founded in 1931 by a small group of Scots concerned at the growing threat to the country's natural and built heritage. Now, it is an influential body with more than a hundred diverse properties. Its remit, set out in various Acts of Parliament, is to promote the care and conservation of the Scottish landscape and historic buildings while providing access for the public to enjoy them.

Over 76,000 hectares (187,000 acres) of countryside are in the Trust's care, encompassing farmland and forest, mountain and moor, waterfalls and islands as well as dramatic cliffs, rugged coastline and beautiful gardens. The Trust owns buildings of historical and architectural importance, from castles to cottages; birthplaces of famous Scots and properties rich in social and industrial history.

The future of this heritage depends on the ability of The National Trust for Scotland to meet ever-increasing financial demands. We can do this only with the help of our membership. Please support our valuable work by becoming a member, making a donation or arranging a legacy.